THE EDWIN POEMS

THE EDWIN POEMS

John Zeigler

Copyright © 2007 by John Zeigler.

Library of Congress Control Number: 2007900274
ISBN: Hardcover   978-1-4257-5274-3
                 Softcover   978-1-4257-5272-9

All rights reserved. No part of this book may be reproduced or transmitted in any form or by any means, electronic or mechanical, including photocopying, recording, or by any information storage and retrieval system, without permission in writing from the copyright owner.

This book was printed in the United States of America.

To order additional copies of this book, contact:
Xlibris Corporation
1-888-795-4274
www.Xlibris.com
Orders@Xlibris.com

38727

To
Edwin Davis Peacock
"Eager Wings"

CONTENTS

BEFORE

Meeting (1940) 11
The Golden Bird 13
Dare I? 15
A Memory, Fifty Years Later 17
At Clingman's Dome 19
September Variations 21
To You, Sleeping (1941) 23
Invitation (1943) 25
Anticipation In War Time 27
Letter On A Still Evening (1940) 29
Only Your Touch 31
Reunion, August 14, 1945 33
Thoughts On The Road From Dunedin to Te Anau, N.Z. (1982) 35
In Hampshire Once (1980) 37
The Shropshire Lad At Fifty (1986) 39
Conversation (1990) 41

AFTER

Five Days (1989) 45
Free (1989) 47
For Edwin 49
Summer Request 51
Dawn 53
The Yamaha (1990) 55
Beyond The Screen 57
The Pear 59
Separation 61
Remembering 63
At Wasserburg (1993) 65
Question 67
Difference (1995) 69
A Cure? (1999) 71
Toss (2000) 73

About the Author 75

BEFORE

MEETING

There was nothing strange in the way we met,
Although we each had need of one to dare
Imprisonment in summer's golden net.
A letter from a friend urged us to share
The troubled waters of our single need
And urged a meeting we had never sought:
For neither you nor I could ever feed
Timidity to strangers. As one blind
From birth, I saw that although peril-fraught
Here, now, was all my want of humankind,
Here in the chiseled fineness of a face
Unlined by vows to any market place:
Here was that nature, innocent and free,
That was to give my life a history.

THE GOLDEN BIRD

When I was twenty, I was wild with love.
I sighed and beat upon my breast with rage.
I had no yardstick to take measure of
The golden bird I sought in vain to cage.

Each day was an undoing, all my acts
Charged with a careless ardor that ignored
The questioning word and the world of fact.
The golden bird was all that I adored.

At twenty-eight I thought that I had learned
Enough of wisdom in the years between:
Rapture and passion, fire and ice I spurned.
The golden bird sang on another green.

I was content with the frail word. My pen
Shadowed the glittering bird that sang of fame:
But suddenly I'm wild with love again
And twenty-eight and twenty are the same.

DARE I?

Sea oats and grasses wave,
Ocean is blue
As your eyes and as grave
As your eyes, too.

If I knew what you thought,
I would know what to be:
You whom I always sought
Tell me what your eyes see.

Dare I speak out my heart?
Dare I destroy
Friendship that was to start
Nothing but joy?

Oh, if I dared to say
All that I feel,
I should be night and day
Setting love's seal.

A MEMORY, FIFTY YEARS LATER

The moon was a great white smile in the summer night,
Its glow sifting down through the shadowy trees
That lined the racing mountain stream. The boulders
Summoned us for leaping and playing at childhood.
Naked, we shouted, sang arias without beginning or end,
Fell, finally, for the first time, into each other's arms
As natural as moon, rocks, water, and knew that
Together all was possible, that we had found an island
In that marvelous August evening of our birth
From which no rescue was desired, or even possible.

AT CLINGMAN'S DOME

Gold shook through the air, a treasure
Scattered by the benevolent sun,
Falling slowly through reds and pale yellows
Tempered by weathers and swift seasons,
As we were, in that rare September
Flowing through us like the shimmering light.
What had begun as a search for oneness
Showed us that mountains, trees, clouds,
Had their moods, too, their separateness,
Yet knew a harmony balancing the whole.
Nothing experienced since that late afternoon
In the noble forest at Clingman's Dome
Has been so profoundly ours, so filled with peace
Enclosing us in its many-colored mantle.

SEPTEMBER VARIATIONS

I
Imprisoned in September
is that day in summer when
a door opened and the heart,
fastidious gentleman, sleep-
walking in an enormous sunset,
woke, rustling the grasses
in a new country, sending
great birds into the color's eye.

II
Like a long-legged boy
Riding the indifferent wave
Before he spills
I came to love.

Tasting the brine
as the sea exploded
I hit the shore with force
that frightened for all time
the skittering creatures
asylumed in my blood.

III
Could we be won by butterflies
As we saw them in September
drifting over the dunes toward the sea
and hovering as we bathed,
all strengths defeated by that flag
torn into yellow flutterings
that shattered into bits the fierce
blue armament of afternoon?

TO YOU, SLEEPING

Lie with your arm across my breast.
Sleep your sweet gentle sleep. Let night
Scatter her starry seed upon the sky.
You who are orient and west
Sleep gently after your delight.

Dream your untroubled dreams and smile
Your slow dreaming smile. Wake not. Sleep
Under the streamers of the moon
That through the windows come. Beguile
The moonlight with your sleeping smile.

Lie with your arm across my breast.
Sleep while you may. Time cannot keep
Us folded here against the hour that soon
Into each waking room must creep
Like some bold, uninvited guest.

INVITATION

Let us go out before the snow begins,
Walk in the grayness by the water's edge,
Kicking old waterworn gray stones
Until we reach the wooded cliff's ledge
Where the foaming water spins.

Let us walk in the forest, damp with color
Of spruce and hemlock and the small ferns
Pointing above the green and russet mosses:
The fire in the alder willow thicket burns
In the youngest branches while the sky grows duller.

There is no need for any affirming word:
That we walk in the woods together is more
Joy than is ever held in searching speech.
A stream is a careless sound on the forest floor
And a singing high in a tree is a single bird.

Let us go out, for soon the snow will start,
A white meadow drifting out of the sky,
And I will show you places never shared
By two who walked together: you and I
Shall be the first to touch the deep wood's heart.

ANTICIPATION IN WAR TIME

And shall we be together in some place
Where the sun shines and pigeons stir bright leaves
On pebbled walks, sharing their rustling grace
With children and the old man who believes
They know him only? Or shall we find
Theaters, city streets, where lost in noise
We find a singleness that serves to bind
Us in one cloth: so, separate from the joys
Of all the others, ignorant of their ills,
We would have nothing but this single love
That like a river flows and swiftly fills
The valley of our separation? Dove,
Wheeling in innocence through Spring's sharp air,
Become the symbol of the life we share.

LETTER ON A STILL EVENING

It is the stillest time I've ever seen:
The sea is pool-calm, and the glaciers lie
No higher than gray turf beneath the lean
Dark shaggy mountains and a pale blue sky.
The bluff stands like a prow above the beach
Where no waves seem to break. Rooted in the snow
The dark heights of the spruce and hemlock reach
Heavenward in the lilac afterglow.

I have come out to see the quiet place,
The lone star hanging in the northern air,
The sharpened rocks as delicate as lace,
The sterner landscape where the fields are bare:
And I am part of all the stillness, too,
Who stand and watch and feel at one with you.

ONLY YOUR TOUCH

Whether the wind touch me,
Or the salmonberry
Or the devil's club
Blocking the narrow path,
I never know.

Only your touch
Holds me upon the hilltop,
Holds me where meadow rue
Lies at my feet for trampling.

Only your touch,
Known in another year,
Holds me forever in that gray unrest
That the blind know
When the sun is warm on their cheeks
And their dark, dark eyes.

REUNION, AUGUST 14, 1945

I
The morning opens like a flower,
The heart becomes a summer rose,
The news is spread in golden notes
On every wind that blows:
Like music from a million throats
The golden singing flows.

II
Over the harbor the clouds
Like women singing with lifted throats
To their young lovers:

In your gray eyes
All of the answers
To all of the questions
I will never ask.

THOUGHTS ON THE ROAD FROM DUNEDIN TO TE ANAU, N.Z.

Sometimes there is a place that seems to be
Waiting for you. No crowds line the streets,
No band is standing by to announce you.
Tables are not set with the best china,
Nor are the children washed clean behind the ears.
The land is there in a fabled, deep serenity,
Sheep grazing, lambs newly tossed on the green
Rolling hills, while in the distance, thrust
Into the cloud-besotted blue, grave mountains
Look upon the landscape with benign authority
As their waterfalls, like errant thoughts,
Come tumbling from the heights or tripping
Through fern glades, now seen, now vanishing.

IN HAMPSHIRE ONCE

In Hampshire once, we saw the hounds
Tethered and restless as the hunt
Gathered on terraced stones, the sounds
Of eagerness crossed by the blunt
Clop of a horse's heels, its old
Rider, a woman, short and trim,
The constant in this game unrolled
Across the hills, up to the rim
Of blue horizon where there stood
A little copse of greening wood.

We downed our port, the hunters' red
Blazed out like trumpets: turning, they
Lit up a country lane and spread
On high into the flawless day.
Along the verge, the crocus shook
Their shimmering heads, bold daffodils
Outlined the edges of the brook
That tumbled down in lilting rills:
The manor house astride the rise
Anchored the landscape to the skies.

The hunt began: we took the road
That led to home and morning tea,
Speaking to country folk who showed
More interest in the harmony
Of nature as this Spring began
Than in the huntsmen on the hill
Or their impatient hounds that ran
In frenzy but with man-taught skill,
Searching the vulnerable hare
As strength seeks weakness everywhere.

THE SHROPSHIRE LAD AT FIFTY

At fifty, The Shropshire Lad, gray hair stirred
By the autumn breeze at his window seat,
Victorian beard the signature of his pride,
Captivates the rest of us with his aloneness.
At his pub in Ludlow one spring evening,
He bought a raffle ticket: now he's in New Zealand,
Fine camera snapping at every stop, old courtesy
Implicit in every move. What does he think
Of the old Japanese with his two granddaughters,
The plump mother from South Africa exhorting us
To travel before it's too late, the Chinese girl
From Canada on her way to Australia after
Waiting on tables in Christchurch? And the rest
Of us with nothing special to set us apart
In the brilliance of the unfolding landscape?
At breakfast we ask him to share our table.
We are curious but we don't ask questions,
Not even to learn his name. He is The Shropshire Lad
Seeing for the first time the great sprawling world
Beyond the Severn. His clear and innocent eyes
Might be our own some forty years ago.

CONVERSATION

I met that special one
Who had that instant claim
And all of life was fun
And nothing was the same.

From day to day there ran
A current swift as sin:
I'd found the only man
To make my senses spin.

The years brought graying hair,
Dark spots upon the skin:
There was no time to spare
For Death was closing in.

And now, what's there to say?
We loved, we had our way.

AFTER

FIVE DAYS

It was a hot summer, August
With pale beginnings, ominous,
Presaging a vague disaster.
In the mountains a peace prevailed,
Calm as the cool, still nights,
Trees hovering in indifference,
The stars without guile,
Friends sweet as water captured
From the bowered streams.
Five days of grace, pure as the days
When my life began on that island
Circled by the sea and green marsh.
Five days of preparation for the years
That would stretch ahead, unnumbered,
As August beat your flailing wings to earth.

FREE

In Georgia's earth there lies
Safe in eternity
Death's calculated prize.
In that austerity,
The spirit life adored
Cannot be bound. The wings
That in compulsion soared
Lift, and the bold wind sings
As waiting sky takes home
Its son, now free to roam.

FOR EDWIN

Like some great playful fish of the sea
Or a winged strength cleaving the air
While we moved at a snail's pace on firm earth,
You went through your life, always sure
That water was there to swim through,
Thunderstorms never to be evaded, a test
Only of wings that were given at birth.
In the stillness that has fallen over us,
Although we have lost a focus for our vision,
There stirs in the emptiness a breath fighting
To become a life worthy of that gift
Bestowed as freely as the sun's warmth
Or the benign beauty of the rising moon.

SUMMER REQUEST

Hear me,
If you are anywhere,
If you exist
Beyond your shallow grave
In some eternal sphere
Where is no list
Of hero or of knave,
Where all are free.

Teach me,
If any power lies
In soul's domain,
How to face morning's light
Wherein the sun's surprise
Lays bare the plain
On which relentless blight
Feasts endlessly.

Calm me,
That all my rage, austere
And desperate,
Become serene as stone;
That I have grace to bear
The summer's weight
Firming within the bone
Our history.

DAWN

In the narrow space between blind and sill,
The horizontal, pale December dawn
Awaits my morning eyes. All's cold and still.
The room in which I slept is slowly drawn
Into another day, as I am, who
Last saw, stretched out upon a floor of stones,
That great chest without breath, loved face that grew
Wan as this morning's light that chills my bones.

THE YAMAHA

Is it reasonable to keep
The upright Yamaha, the first
Object bought for our first house,
Standing as black as the quick death
That made it mute? In its long sleep
Has music hovered there like thirst
That needs quenching, or fire? To douse
That flame would take my blood, my breath.

It has its wall; it's straight and sleek
And mirrors on its surface me,
Sitting close to an empty chair.
At times I think it knows something
I need to learn, something I seek
From pictures, furniture, to be
Open for striking, more aware
Of life's angles than its ring:
Of possibilities, of sounds
Waiting to be born, without bounds.

BEYOND THE SCREEN

Beyond the screen, where shadows gambol
On the green lawn and gentle winds play
In the leaves of apricot and pear, birds dart
With or without mates, uttering old cries
Of love or wonder or alarm. A rose you planted
Twenty years ago offers a disturbing
Solitary note of color on its aging branch.
To come to terms with that resplendent bud
Takes more time than the afternoon permits,
For there are groceries to buy, errands to be run,
And contemplation leads me round and round
With thoughts like spokes upon a broken wheel
While dry necessity burns bridges to the past.

THE PEAR

There will be a mist of white
against the old wall of my neighbor.
Against that brick wall of my being
no pears blossom;
Ragged branches speak of a winter burden
no feasting squirrel will find appealing.
For them there will be a banquet
of green fruit, never ripe.
Is there a way to eat grey twigs
anticipating April,
Or are those branches always March,
never to show a leaf, a flower
although the promise is always there?

SEPARATION

How slowly the days drift,
Leaving a continent
To be an island, clear-
Cut and definite, where
New species will be born,
Links with the past be sure,
Submerged in what never
Was before, as *something*
Struggles to become free.

REMEMBERING

Remembering mountains
Where we clambered,
Tumbling into gullies,
Pulling at branches,
Testing rocks in streams
Where we bathed at dusk
Before striving for sleep
Beside twig fires or in
Lean-tos come upon by chance;
Leaping into the ferny morning
Drunk on the still beauty
Of ancient wilderness,
Two spirits that wanted life
To be a never-ending exploration,
A soaring into the unexpected,
A sharing that must be absolute,
I know that we kept true
To that first testing, that
First run into a future
Stretching endlessly.

AT WASSERBURG

Worms of light crawl through the weeping birch
Telling me, cheer up, it's not that dark.
I sit on a bench while the tourists search
For something to remember. A dog's bark
Causes a head or two to turn, a lad
To laugh as though wishing the hand that drags
Him through this hot, dumb morning had
Been snapped at, bitten. No one ever lags
Behind, although the village is too small
For loss. I watch them in their sturdy shoes,
Their shorts, a flowering skirt or two. All
Wear as their armor cameras. I choose
A couple, unencumbered, old and frail,
To be my allies in this search for—what?
For figures in that ancient fairy tale,
My life? Or what *that* only scuttlebutt?

QUESTION

Whatever became of Time
That pulled us on a string
Into the calm future?
Has it become suture
Binding the riven wing
Cleansed of its earthly grime?
Of course it's always there
And I am always here.

Whatever became of Love
That rose into the air
Like some enormous bird
Clamoring to be heard?
Its song was everywhere
Until death's bloody glove
Struck quickly, unobserved.
Of course it's always there
And I am always here.

When Time and Love have flown
And death devoured light,
Infrequently there comes,
But not with rolling drums,
A bursting into sight
Of recreated dawn.
And now you're always here
And I am always there.

DIFFERENCE

What is this pretending
But a fear of living
With all the added weight
That comes with truth, like spate
Of freshets bringing stones
To fling against our bones?

Sometimes, when one survives
The mockery in eyes,
The battering inflections,
Answering questions
No one has asked, a slow
Silence begins to flow.

The disciplines we find
Are always there to bind.
Talk withers on the lips:
Anxieties, like whips,
Beat on the restless flesh
Wherein our feelings mesh.

We live from birth to age
Between our joy and rage
And then, in that last breath
We learn from robber death
Which breaches every wall
That constancy is all.

A CURE?

Remember the four year old
falling out of the chinaberry tree,
the rusty nail waiting
like a punishment?

And then, immobile, almost,
in that small white bed,
the neighbor crossing the field
with warm waffles,
the small sisters crawling
around the bed, laughing?

Finally, the young doctor
lifting you in his coated arms
and placing you beside him
in the old buggy, setting off
along unknown lanes with trees
like wind-blown umbrellas overhead
in a search for healing weeds,
mysteriously spotted, gathered?

The unknown. That was my first
awareness of the great world
I would travel later, carrying
with me a nail's danger, that
doctor, that buggy, that search
for what could, perhaps, be found,
a cure.

TOSS

Toss, toss the redundant baggage
Into the undirected winds
That it may be lost on far plains
Or buried in other jungles.
Learn from a Yeats or a Serkin
What to hold on to, what renounce,
So that those last bold energies,
Like pure water running over pure stones,
Shape at the end a lean triumphant Art.

ABOUT THE AUTHOR

A South Carolinian, born 5 February 1912, educated in Florence and at The Citadel, John Zeigler has lived in Charleston, his ancestral home, since 1946, when he co-founded The Book Basement, an intimate bookshop specializing in Caroliniana. At The Citadel, he began and was editor of *The Shako*, the school's literary magazine. After graduation, while working at The R.F.C. in Washington, D.C., he was editor of the little magazine *Foothills*, which introduced the early work of many young writers, one of whom was the gifted Jessamyn West. While serving in the Navy during the Second World War, he was stationed for an extended period at Yakutat Bay, Alaska, an experience which resulted in some of the work in this volume.

His poetry has been seen in such periodicals and newspapers as *The American Mercury, Harper's Bazaar, The Lyric, Good Housekeeping, Nature Magazine, Christian Science Monitor, New York Times, New York Herald Tribune, Washington Post, The Poetry Society of South Carolina Yearbook* and others. His book of poetry, *Alaska and Beyond*, was published in 1984.

The poems in this collection were written during John Zeigler's 49-year partnership with Edwin Peacock, whom he met in 1940 after receiving a letter from a cousin of Carson McCullers urging that he meet her friend, then working for the Army at Fort Moultrie while John was spending the summer with an aunt on Sullivan's Island. A year after they met they moved to San Francisco, joined the Navy as Radiomen, and after the war opened the book shop.

Printed in the United States
78832LV00006B/322